A Critique of the Idea of Progress

Ethics, Knowledge and Evolution

Robert Nicholls

123 Books

Copyright © 2011 by Robert Nicholls

All rights reserved. This book, or parts thereof, may not be reproduced in any form without permission.

A catalogue record for this book is available from the British Library

ISBN: 978-1-907962-23-3

Published by 123 Books

Reading, England

For John

Flight is the only truly new sensation that men have achieved in modern history

James Dickey

Contents

Preface — 9

Introduction — 11

1 What is the Object of Progress? — 13

2 What is the Subject of Progress? — 19

3 The Progressive Modification of the Nonliving by the Living — 23

4 Progress and Striving — 28

5 The Existence of Striving — 35

6 Conclusion — 46

Preface

The aim of this book is to consider the idea of progress. It is clear to me that progress is a concept of key importance to human society; we like to feel that we are progressing as a species. But what exactly does it mean to progress? And how does progress in the human realm fit into the bigger picture? Does progress in the human realm have a wider significance by fitting into a larger picture of progress at the level of the planet Earth? If so, does human progress also have significance at the level of the entire universe? These are the issues which I will be considering in this book.

Introduction

The idea of progress has been around for thousands of years. In this period there have been several different ideas about what it is that actually progresses. Despite these differences the idea of progress is usually restricted to the human species, and in particular, to human culture. In this book I argue that progress can be more accurately conceived of as a phenomenon that concerns life as a whole and not just the human species.

In *Chapter One* I consider the question: What is the object of progress? That is to say – what is it that is progressing? Is it ethics? Is it knowledge? Or, is it something else? In *Chapter Two* I consider the question: What is the subject of progress? In other words – which part of the universe instantiates the object of progress? Is it the human species? Is it life? Or, is it the entire universe? In the remaining chapters I present my own view of progress – a view that takes the object of progress to be life as a whole.

Chapter 1

What is the Object of Progress?

When people talk about progress they are usually talking about some aspect of human culture. The most common view of progress seems to be the idea that humankind has become more ethical over history, is presently becoming more ethical, and will continue to become more ethical in the future. The idea is that over time humanity progresses towards equality and justice, and individuals gradually progress towards becoming the 'ideal human'. As we look back on the twentieth century we can see that it is easy to ridicule this notion that humankind is progressing. We look back and see two world wars, the increasing global pervasiveness of capitalism, and a forever increasing gap between the rich and the poor.

Many would hold that the opposite is true. Isn't it obvious that humanity isn't progressing; rather, isn't humanity degenerating from a state of primordial bliss to a state of ruthless individualism? It can be argued that humans are increasingly isolating themselves from the suffering that they cause and that this leads to a mirage of progress. Hiding behind technology man can now press a button and kill innumerable people on the other side of the world; he can even buy meat from a supermarket and not even realize that it was once a fellow living

What is the Object of Progress?

animal. There seems to be an increasing detachment from the unsavoury elements of human existence as culture advances; we prefer not to see the bloodshed in human war or animal slaughter, but it obviously still exists. Have we really progressed ethically through the development of culture?

Given recent human history it would be difficult to support the view that humankind has either progressed ethically, or will progress ethically in the future. However, there is an alternative view of human progress. This view asserts that progress is not about ethics, it is about the development of human knowledge. It is argued that humanity's knowledge of the world that they are embedded in, and their concordant ability to transform that world for their own purposes, has increased over history, is currently increasing, and will continue to increase into the future. We have one long progression from the primitive tool use of our ancestors, through the enlightenment, the industrial revolution, and to our technological world of today. This is a continuous progression of increasing knowledge and increasing ability to modify the universe which we inhabit.

This is a view of progress that seems to have at least some grains of truth. What is interesting is the way that this knowledge/technological view of progress intertwines with the ethical view of progress. One could hold either that increasing knowledge makes us more ethical, or that increasing

What is the Object of Progress?

knowledge makes us less ethical. In so far as increasing knowledge is accompanied by increasingly advanced technology, it seems that the latter view could be nearer the truth. The increasing pervasiveness of technology leads to an increasing disjoint between action/decision and consequence, a disjoint that leads to a distancing from giving the ethical elements of actions and decisions their full weight.

I take it to be obvious that progress of human knowledge has occurred, is occurring, and will continue to occur into the foreseeable future. I also take it as obvious that this knowledge has resulted in progress in terms of humankind's ability to modify the world. This modification ability has increased throughout the past, is still increasing, and will continue to increase into the foreseeable future. I find these to be very sound and unproblematic assertions. However, they are the basis of further claims that I wish to defend that one might find to be less sound.

Chapter 2

What is the Subject of Progress?

We have already noted that the progress debate has focused on the human species. The starting premise to the debate has been that the subject of progress is humankind. However, it is possible to believe that there could be an alternative subject of progress. The true entity of progression could be 'life'. The history of progress, current progress, and future progress could all concern the increasing modification of the world by life; this would be a progression that goes back to the dawn of life. If this is the case, then extrapolating that small segment of life that is the human species misses the bigger picture of progress.

A corollary of this expanded view of progress is a further claim which also contradicts contemporary conventional wisdom. If the true nature of progress is the increasing modification of the non-living by *life as a whole*, then it follows that there is directedness in the evolutionary process; there is a striving for greater control of the non-living, a striving that if successful ultimately reaches a technological species such as humankind. It is currently fashionable to believe that the evolution of life is directionless, dictated by the interplay of environmental niches and natural selection. It follows from this view that a technological species evolves as a 'fluke'. However

What is the Subject of Progress?

much evidence accrues that the whole history of life is a progression of increasing modification of the non-living by the living as a whole, many will still hold that the evolution of mankind is a fluke, and the fact that we became a technological species is a further fluke. But if life as a whole is the *subject* of progress and its *object* is increasing modification of the nonliving, then this dominant view of directionless evolution is clearly false.

When technological progress is viewed from a purely anthropocentric perspective it is possible to ask whether technological progress is a good thing or a bad thing. We can weigh the benefits of technology such as medicine and telecommunications against the negative aspects such as pollution and climate change. However, when technological progress is viewed from the wider perspective of the progressive modification of the nonliving by the living then the question of whether it is good or bad becomes redundant. It becomes the case that such progress is simply a reflection of the fundamental nature of life. One can argue about whether the fact that the universe is constructed in such a way would make it preferable that it didn't exist, but it seems more sensible to just accept that this is the way the universe actually is, and to reject the notion that the universe is intrinsically good or bad.

Chapter 3

The Progressive Modification of the Nonliving by the Living

I have proposed that the view of progress as a continuous increase in the ability of humankind to modify the nonhuman could be just a partial segment of a bigger picture. The bigger picture could be the progressive modification of the nonliving by the *living as a whole*. From this wider perspective we get a very different perspective on the technological progress of humankind.

The narrow anthropocentric view of technological progress increasingly views technology as a bad thing. The pervasiveness and advanced nature of technology since the industrial revolution is asserted to have had a number of increasingly deleterious side-effects. These include a range of modifications to the planetary environment that are believed to be initiating a human-induced 'environmental crisis' – these are chiefly *climate change* which arises from extensive fossil fuel use and deforestation; and, an *increasing loss of biodiversity* arising from an over-exploitation of resources and habitat modification.

There are still a minority of people who deny that the human species has significantly altered the planetary environmental conditions. This view seems to be obviously wrong – we have adequate scientific knowledge of how the atmosphere and carbon dioxide sinks work to know for certain that we have significantly changed the environment. In fact, it is not even a question of science. It is simply a brute fact that every living thing modifies its environment in virtue of being a living thing. And it also straightforwardly follows that humankind has *increasingly* modified the planetary environment throughout history because of two incontrovertible factors – the human population explosion, and our increasing use of technology.

Having said this, when technological progress is viewed from the wider perspective of the progressive modification of the nonliving by the living, then human technology becomes just the cutting edge of a process that has been ongoing for billions of years.

A Critique of the Idea of Progress

How are we to view the 'environmental crisis' of modernity from this wider perspective? From our wider perspective the changes humanity has made to the environment are neither good nor bad, they simply reflect the nature of life, and its strivings to increasingly modify the non-living in order to survive.

On first hearing this argument one might find it to be quite absurd. We are increasingly told that humankind is the *cause* of a global environmental crisis that will lead to a mass extinction of species, including in all likelihood our own species. Scientists tell us that when we disrupt the environment too much several 'tipping points' will be passed and planetary climatic conditions will jump to a new more stable set – a set that is not conducive for the continued existence of the human species.

However, from our wider perspective of viewing technological progress from the perspective of life as a whole, we can immediately see that these scientists miss the bigger picture. From this perspective we can see that humankind are not the initiators of harm to the rest of life, they are, rather, the leading edge of the progressive modification of the nonliving by the living.

Chapter 4

Progress and Striving

I have suggested that the *subject* of progress could be life, and that the *object* of progress could be the progressive modification of the nonliving. If this is so, then it seems that we have to envision life as a whole as engaged in a continuous 'striving' for survival. The nonliving world can be a very inhospitable place to live. We currently live in a period of relative environmental stability, but in the past the progression of life has been seriously threatened by both the eruption of supervolcanoes and massive meteor impacts. The universe is in a continuous state of flux, whilst life requires a very specific set of environmental conditions in order to exist and flourish. We would, therefore, expect, if life has an inbuilt striving to survive, that when life arises that it acts in such a way as to maintain the conditions that it requires against the backdrop of the nonliving flux.

In fact, this is what we see on the Earth. Life has maximised its chances of survival by filling every possible niche and by progressively modifying the nonliving. Life as a whole has been regulating planetary conditions for hundreds of millions of years, keeping the Global Mean Surface Temperature (GMST) at just the right level for more complex life-forms to evolve. Any significant deviation in the

GMST from fifteen degrees Centigrade and life cannot evolve more complex forms, and is thereby doomed to die on the planet.

It has only recently been recognised that a planet has a limited lifespan. Furthermore, there is only a relatively short window which life has, when it arises, to spread out over the whole planet and start regulating the planetary conditions to keep them favourable for its development to more complex forms. If life doesn't achieve this planetary temperature regulation then it is doomed to die because it cannot evolve into more complex forms. The need for more complex forms of life is two-fold.

Firstly, the solar output of the Sun is forever increasing, which means that the attempts of life to regulate the GMST increasingly come under strain over time. Initially carbon dioxide from the atmosphere can be stored underground as decaying vegetation to balance the increasing solar input. However, as the Sun forever gets hotter and hotter this regulatory system comes under stress. This is why in the past million years the planet has gone through a period of instability which is revealed by repeated transitions between Ice Ages and Interglacial Periods. These transitions are triggered by Milankovitch Cycles, but are a relatively recent phenomenon due to the systemic stress caused by the forever increasing output of the Sun. Prior to the last million years the Milankovitch Cycles had no such effects because the regulatory system was not under stress. If there is an inherent striving in life to survive then increasingly complex forms would be striven for. This is because only these forms have the ability to modify the nonliving to such an extent that the GMST can be maintained when the system goes past a given level of stress. In other words, humankind and human technology are the saviours of life, not the initiators of damage to life. Only humankind, if we are able to fulfil our destiny, can save life; saviour requires the development of technology that manages the entire environment of the planet.

Secondly, complex life forms are required because managing the GMST through complex technology is itself only a short-term fix. It gives a window in which more advanced technology can be

Progress and Striving

generated so that life can leave the Earth before the planet becomes totally inhospitable for life. The increasing solar output of the Sun will ultimately destroy all life on the planet, and then the planet itself.

We can feel sympathy with those who cannot see this bigger picture. These people will see technology as a bad thing, as the enemy of life, and will advocate that humankind should revert to a simpler life in which we live in harmony with our surroundings without the use and further development of complex technologies. Despite our sympathy for these people, we have to conclude that if their dreams came to pass then all of life on the planet would be doomed to die in the not too distant future;

this is surely not what they really want to happen. If life is striving for survival it will continue to progressively modify the nonliving via increasingly complex human technological advancements.

Chapter 5

The Existence of Striving

Can it really be the case that *life as a whole* is progressing? Is life striving for survival through planetary regulation and the development of more complex forms that progressively modify the nonliving? We live in a strange age in which science has disenchanted the universe, and the only respectable intellectual position seems to be to hold that everything is meaningless. Those in the clutches of natural selection assert that the evolution of life is an essentially undirected process, that there is no central place for striving. To assert that humankind has some kind of special place in the arena of life; that life strives for a technological species wherever it arises, is regarded as both unscientific and unwarranted.

Nevertheless, there are very good reasons for believing in the existence of striving. If we were to start with the belief that striving exists then we would see it wherever we look. However, when most people look their vision is coloured by their ingrained education which asserted a meaningless, undirected, non-striving evolution of life. It is possible that the true nature of life might reveal itself *directly through itself* and not through a science textbook.

The Existence of Striving

We can attempt to throw off the shackles of our education, and think for ourselves about the nature of life and our experience of it. I am not suggesting that science should not inform our thinking; just that it should not overwhelm our thinking. When we look at the world with fresh eyes, with the knowledge of previous generations in the back of our mind, what do we see? Do we see a world in which life is striving for existence, or a set of essentially meaningless and undirected processes?

Let us start with our own *direct experience* of the world. Whether it is our own body, or the bodies of other people, we observe striking regenerative and healing capacities. The living body itself can be observed striving for survival every time it is injured, ill, or bleeding. Furthermore, we are engaged in a seemingly unstoppable quest to prolong our lives as long as possible, whether through medicine, artificial implants, or even cryogenic freezing. We also directly observe the striving for survival through one of the most dominant drivers of our existence – the sexual drive. The vast majority of people are also naturally disposed to sadness when they observe the premature or unnecessary death of fellow humans or other complex forms of life. The inbuilt striving for life and the intrinsic goodness of prolonging life pervade our entire existence.

When we observe the living world that surrounds us what do we see? Everywhere we see the same striving by *life as a whole* for greater complex-

The Existence of Striving

ity. We observe different species of life competing for the same resources; inevitably the species with the greatest striving ability is the one that comes to dominate, thereby strengthening the survival chances of *life as a whole*. We can examine every part of the planet, from the ocean depths to kilometres below the crust, and everywhere we will find that some part of life has found a way to survive. We can observe the succession of whole ecosystems, in which weaker states *of life as a whole* increasingly become dominated by more robust states of *life as a whole*. As succession occurs ecosystem redundancy increases thereby making the continued existence of life more likely. We see the same striving for survival and the same sexual drive wherever we look.

Against this backdrop what can science tell us about the history of life? Science tells us that life arose approximately 3.6 billion years ago with the emergence of bacteria. By 3 billion years ago these bacteria had formed stromatolites which filled the atmosphere with oxygen so that more complex forms of life could emerge. The strivings of the bacteria were creating the conditions that enabled them to form more complex life via the temporary formation of stromatolites. This process took until 2.2 billion years ago when the continual strivings of 1.4 billion years led to the formation of the stratospheric ozone layer. The formation of this layer by life was a necessary perquisite for it to reach more complex forms, because it enabled the formation of eukaryotic cell-based land animals. By 1.6 billion years ago eukaryotic cells had formed in the oceans, by 1 billion years ago they had formed algae, and by 530 million years ago they formed a plethora of marine animals.

All of these strivings to greater complexity enabled life to colonise the land 400 million years ago. At this stage the land animals and plants were the leading edge of the strivings of *life as a whole*. Plants and animals engaged in a mutually cooperative venture in which plants produced oxygen for animals, and animals produced carbon dioxide for plants. *Life as a whole* was progressing towards forever greater complexity aided by all of its constituent parts. *Life as a whole* was also regulating the planetary conditions to maintain them at a level which enabled the further progression of life. This progression led to the evolution of tool users, and ultimately to the technological species of humankind.

Let us return to our earlier question: Do we see a world in which life is striving for existence, or a set of essentially meaningless and undirected processes? It certainly appears that we can observe the striving for existence all around us, and that everything we know about the evolution of life suggests that it is one long progression of striving for complexity. Many will be unconvinced and will assert that the evolution of complex life and of humankind is a purely fortuitous event. However, this is a largely unfounded assertion; a belief without supporting evidence.

In the previous chapter we saw that if there was a striving for existence then, because of the limited life of the Earth, increasingly complex forms of life would need to be striven for. Furthermore, this complexity would need to reach a technological species. When we contemplate the evolution of life from bacteria to stromatolites, to eukaryotic cells, to simple marine animals, to simple land animals, to complex land animals, and ultimately to the human species, we see that exactly this process has occurred. We also need to remember that just like the stromatolites which enabled humankind to come into existence, the human body itself is an arrangement of diverse bacteria.

The existence of the striving of *life as a whole* for survival should really be beyond any serious doubt. One can always believe that everything that happens is just a fluke, simply a whole series of fortuitous events. However, thoughtful contemplation of our nature, the world around us, and the evolution of life, can all lead one to a very different conclusion. Perhaps the conclusion that the *oxygen formation* of stromatolites and the *technology formation* of humans are part of one and the same process will leave many people feeling uncomfortable. Perhaps they *should* feel uncomfortable about this; being at the leading edge of the progressive modification of the nonliving by the living doesn't necessarily lend itself to a happy existence. Indeed, going back to the start of the book, we saw that the technological nature of human existence could be a factor in our lack of ethical progress, and our degeneration from a state of primordial bliss.

Chapter 6

Conclusion

I have considered various ideas concerning the object of progress and the subject of progress. I have contended that human society is progressing because of the ever increasing knowledge of the universe that human society is acquiring. This increasing knowledge is intertwined with another process – the utilisation of the increasing store of knowledge by the human species to progressively modify its surroundings.

I have located this progress at the level of human society within a larger evolutionary process in which the whole of life is progressively modifying its surroundings. So, on this view the human species, through its technological ability, can be seen as the leading edge of the progressive modification of the nonliving by the living. I have also contended that when one looks at the world with fresh eyes one can see life striving to survive through modifying its surroundings almost everywhere one looks. Life on Earth has, ever since it first arose, been progressing – it has been increasingly gaining the ability to modify its surroundings – and the human species is the pinnacle of this evolutionary process. As this process continues in the future the ability of life to modify its surroundings will continue to increase via increasing human knowledge and the associated increasingly complex human technologies.

www.ingramcontent.com/pod-product-compliance
Lightning Source LLC
Chambersburg PA
CBHW061302040426
42444CB00010B/2481